Table of Contents

List of Included Forms

Overview

The purpose of this handbook is to help you manage the use of multiple assessments, interpret the results, and then use that information for instructional planning. It will provide you with basic definitions and clear guidance on how test scores can be a useful resource for addressing your students' needs.

What is assessment?

- Assessment is the process of systematically gathering evidence about what students know and can do.

- Assessments can be both formal and informal as long as the information is systematically collected, scored, and recorded.

Macmillan/McGraw-Hill Treasures Assessments

The assessments included within the program will help you gather data to address students' instructional needs.

Our assessment options are...

- Grounded in research
- Compliant with the No Child Left Behind framework
- Based on studies of reliability and validity
- Aligned with standards
- Aligned with K-6 curriculum
- Easy to manage
- Designed to minimize testing time

	Assessment Options			
Assessment	**Purpose**	**What It Does**	**When to Give It**	**How to Give It**
Screening, Diagnostic, Placement Assessment	**Screening:** • DIBELS* (K-3) • TPRI* (K-3) • Oral Reading Fluency (4-6)	Identifies students at possible risk of reading failure	Beginning, Middle, and End of Year	Administer individually
	Diagnostic: • TPRI* (K-3) • Fox in a Box* (K-2) • Informal Reading Inventory (1-6)	Identifies students' specific strengths and weaknesses for instructional planning and grouping	After screening and when additional diagnostic information is needed	Administer individually
	Placement: • Placement Tests (K-6) * Alignment to **TREASURES** included in this book	Places students into appropriate grade levels and instructional groups	Beginning of year and with new entrants	Whole group; Administer individually in Grade K, and as needed in Grades 1-6

Assessment Options

Assessment	Purpose	What It Does	When to Give It	How to Give It
Fluency Assessment	Progress Monitoring Formative	Determines if students are reading accurately and fluently	Every 2-3 weeks for most students	Administer individually
Running Records, Including Benchmark Books	Diagnostic Progress Monitoring Formative	Determines instructional reading levels by identifying students' reading strategies and analyzing miscues	Every 3-4 weeks	Administer individually
Weekly Assessment	Progress Monitoring Formative	Identifies students' strengths and weaknesses for instructional planning and grouping	At the end of a week of instruction	Whole group
Unit Assessment	Progress Monitoring/ Formative Outcome/ Summative	Identifies students' strengths and weaknesses for instructional planning and grouping	At the end of five weeks of instruction	Whole group
Benchmark Assessment	Progress Monitoring Formative	Measures students' progress and growth	Beginning, Middle, and End of Year	Whole group

This book includes the following assessments:

- Screening assessment information
- Diagnostic assessments
- Oral Reading Fluency passages
- Informal Reading Inventory passages
- Placement Tests

What is a Screening Assessment?

These are brief assessments that are individually administered and do not take a lot of time. They allow you to identify which students are at risk of reading failure by separating students into two groups:

- those who need additional instruction on the tested skills;
- those who do not.

How to interpret the results

- If a student does need additional instruction on the tested skills, as indicated by a low test score, then administer a Diagnostic test to identify which specific skills need to be addressed. This group of students is sometimes called *students at risk of academic failure.*

- If a student does *not* need additional instruction on the tested skills, as indicated by a high score on the Screening test, then there is no need to administer a Diagnostic assessment. Move right into the core reading instruction. These students are, most likely, reading at or above grade level.

- Sometimes districts or state departments require all students to take a Diagnostic test. If this requirement exists, then there is really no need to administer a Screening test. Begin with the Diagnostic assessment to paint a thorough picture of a student's academic reading strengths and weaknesses.

Screening Assessment Option for K-3

Your state and/or district may have identified a screening assessment for you to use with your students, such as **DIBELS** or **TPRI**. It is recommended that you use your approved screening assessment as it aligns with **TREASURES**.

DIBELS (Dynamic Indicators of Basic Early Literacy Skills)

Description

Use for **screening** and **progress monitoring**. These are short, one-minute fluency measures that identify students at risk of reading difficulties.

- Initial Sound Fluency (K)
- Phoneme Segmentation Fluency (K-1)
- Word Use Fluency (K-3)
- Nonsense Word Fluency (K-1)
- Letter Naming Fluency (K-1)
- Oral Reading and Retell Fluency (1-3)

How to administer: Administer the tests individually.

When to administer

Beginning, middle, and end of the year for **screening** (see chart below). For **progress monitoring** between screening periods, administer every two weeks for students identified as *some risk*, and every six weeks for students at *low risk*.

DIBELS Link to TREASURES

When to Screen	Kindergarten	Grades 1-3
Beginning of the Year	Smart Start	Unit 1
Middle of the Year	Unit 4	Unit 3
End of the Year	Unit 9	Unit 5

Teacher Tips

Read the DIBELS Administration and Scoring Guide. Have the materials, clipboard, and stopwatch ready. Use benchmark probes for screening, and progress monitoring probes to evaluate reading growth.

For information about ordering DIBELS, go to http://dibels.uoregon.edu/.

Screening/Diagnostic Assessment Option for K-3

TPRI (Texas Primary Reading Inventory)

Description

Use for **screening, diagnostic**, and **progress monitoring**. These short probes measure **Graphophonemic Knowledge** and **Phonemic Awareness (K-1)**, and **Word Reading (1-3)**, and identify students *not* at risk of reading failure. These are the **diagnostic**, or *Inventory*, subtests:

- **Book and Print Awareness (K)**
- **Phonemic Awareness (K-1)**
- **Listening Comprehension (K-1)**
- **Graphophonemic Knowledge (K-3)**
- **Reading Accuracy (1-3)**
- **Reading Fluency (1-3)**
- **Reading Comprehension (1-3)**

How to administer: Administer individually; follow Branching Rules.

When to administer

Beginning, middle, and end of the year for the **Screening** *(see chart below)* and **Inventory** assessments. For **progress monitoring**, use the Fluency Kit (1-3), Progress Monitoring tool (K-1), and TPRI Kit with all students.

TPRI Link to Treasures

When to Screen	Kindergarten	Grades 1-3
Beginning of the Year	Start mid-year	Unit 1
Middle of the Year	Unit 4	Unit 3
End of the Year	Unit 9	Unit 5

Teacher Tips

Have all the materials ready. Use a standard pronunciation for all sounds. Use the Intervention Skills Guide for additional activities to target specific skills.

© Macmillan/McGraw-Hill

For more information go to www.tpri.org. To order, call 1-800-442-9685

Screening Assessment Option for 4-6

Oral Reading Fluency

Description

This screening assessment identifies children who may require diagnostic testing and additional instructional support to meet grade-level expectations. There are fiction and nonfiction oral reading fluency passages with explicit and implicit comprehension questions. Student performance is measured by having students do a timed reading of the selected passage. The number of words correct per minute is the oral fluency rate.

Pages 25-63

How to administer

The student reads a passage while you record any errors on the fluency record sheet. Be sure to start your stopwatch when the student reads the first word. Afterwards, the student answers the comprehension questions orally. Calculate the student's words correct per minute rate and check it against the Oral Reading Fluency Norms chart on page 27 in the **Screening, Diagnostic, Placement Assessment** book. If a student's WCPM score falls more than ten points below the benchmarks shown on the chart, the student is not reading fluently.

When to administer

Administer the assessment at the beginning, middle, and end of the year.

Teacher Tips

Have each student read at least two passages to evaluate reading performance. It is essential to consider both the norms-based fluency rate and the student's comprehension to determine if further testing and instructional intervention is necessary.

What is a Diagnostic Assessment?

- A test administered to those students who appear to be at risk of failing to read, or need additional reading instruction.

- A detailed assessment that pinpoints a student's strengths and weaknesses.

- A test that includes several items, and often requires a minimum of one hour to administer. Some Diagnostic tests for young students can be given in sections on consecutive days.

- A test that can be group or individually administered, depending on the test and the age of the student.

How to interpret the results

- A screening test will tell you, for example, that a student has a weakness in comprehension. A diagnostic test shows you that the student understands what the words mean, but has trouble remembering the sequence of events in a story. From this information you know that you need to provide additional instruction in the comprehension strategy "identify sequence of events."

- Use the information to help you form small, flexible groups.

Diagnostic Assessment Option for K-2

Your state and/or district may have identified a diagnostic assessment for you to use with your students, such as **Fox in a Box** or **TPRI**. It is recommended that you use your approved diagnostic assessment as it aligns with **TREASURES**.

Fox in a Box

Description

The kit includes standardized and systematic literacy activities to **diagnose** students' skills in the areas of Phonemic Awareness, Phonics, Reading and Oral Expression, and Listening and Writing. There are benchmark levels for each developmentally-appropriate activity. The fox puppet helps make the assessment child friendly.

How to administer

Individually and whole group; record results in a Literacy Progress Record (LPR) which then travels with the student from year to year. Refer to the flow chart in the Teacher's Guide for guidance on how to administer the activities.

When to administer

Administer in early fall and early spring, or more frequently to use as a **progress monitoring** tool. There are specific performance benchmarks and mastery dates to help you plan.

Teacher Tips

Before beginning, familiarize yourself with the activity and gather the necessary materials. Record results directly in the student's LPR, and be sure to include the date when the skill was mastered. Assess all of the children in the same activity before going on to a new activity.

For more information about ordering Fox in a Box, go to www.ctb.com

Diagnostic Assessment Option for 1-6

IRI (Informal Reading Inventory)

Pages 66-128

Description

Use the IRI as a **diagnostic** to gather information about a student's comprehension and reading accuracy. The IRI measures three reading levels: independent, instructional, and frustrational. There are two fiction and two nonfiction passages per grade level. The passages are to be used for either oral or silent reading. There are five questions per passage to assess the student's comprehension: three literal, one vocabulary, and one interpretive.

How to administer

Administer the assessment individually; start with the Grade 1 Word List to determine grade-level placement. Students who make two errors should go back to the previous list and start reading at that level. The correct instructional level is the one where the student misses only one word. This is the level the student should begin reading at. Refer to the Code for Marking Word Recognition Errors on page 69 in the **Screening, Diagnostic, Placement Assessment** book to help you mark the scoring sheet for each passage.

When to administer

Use the IRI as a diagnostic tool after screening.

Teacher Tips

Always have the reading passages, recording sheets, and graded word lists ready before beginning. Use both the oral and silent passages to determine a student's reading level. In order to administer the IRI efficiently, you should be familiar with directions, passages, and questions.

Placement Tests for K-6

Placement Tests

Description

The **Placement Tests** include passages and items that assess comprehension, vocabulary, word recognition, phonics, and other skills. Students who achieve a total test score of 70%-90% should receive on level reading instruction. Students who score higher than 90% should receive some beyond level instruction. Students who score lower than 70% should receive approaching level instruction. Students who show a pattern of low scores on this and other assessments should be evaluated for the **Reading Triumphs** Intervention Program.

Pages 129-253

How to administer

Administer the tests whole class, or individually if needed. The tests take from 35 to 60 minutes to complete, depending on grade level.

When to administer

Administer at the beginning of the year, with new entrants, or when you need additional diagnostic information.

Teacher Tips

For those students whose scores do not clearly define their areas of weaknesses and strengths, administer additional assessments such as the IRI and the Running Records. For students who seem to be significantly above grade level, administer the placement test for the next higher level for additional information.

What is a Progress Monitoring Assessment?

- An informal or formal assessment used to guide instruction.

- A test that is usually quick and easy to administer and score.

- A test that is given individually or in a group.

- A test that is administered frequently: every week, every two weeks, or every six weeks, depending on which specific Progress Monitoring test you select.

- A test that is both systematic and ongoing, with results that are documented and recorded.

How to use the results

- Use the results to help guide instructional decision-making.

- These are **formative** assessments; they provide real information, not just scores or grades. The information should be used to plan future instruction.

- Use the results to provide feedback to students on how they are progressing. This feedback can take the form of written and oral comments related to specific skills, or an analysis of a student's strengths and weaknesses.

Weekly Assessments for 1-6

Weekly Assessment

Description

The **Weekly Assessment** is designed to assess your students' mastery of the skills taught throughout the week. Each week there will be a new passage for students to read. The test questions cover comprehension strategies and skills, vocabulary strategies, grammar, mechanics, usage, and spelling. The passage will be followed by fourteen questions that cover the skills for the week. Use the results of the Weekly Assessment as a formative assessment tool to help monitor student progress. Information gathered by evaluating the results of this assessment can also be used to diagnose specific strengths and weaknesses of your students.

The **Leveled Weekly Assessment** is an alternative assessment at the same instructional reading level as the Approaching Leveled Readers. Students taking the leveled assessment can apply the skills they have learned to text that is at their instructional level. Students reading at an approaching level require additional testing with multiple assessments such as Fluency, IRI, Running Records, and TPRI or DIBELS (K-3). To alleviate over-testing, you have the option of administering this leveled assessment every other week.

How to administer

Distribute copies of the Weekly Assessment, and an Answer Sheet if you choose to use one. Make sure that each student is following the directions and writing responses in the correct places.

When to administer

Administer the Weekly Assessment when you have completed the week of instruction. Administer the Leveled Weekly Assessment at the end of weeks one, three, and five of each unit.

Teacher Tips

Providing students with a new read allows you to assess how well students have mastered the skills for the week. Use this information to help you with instructional planning and grouping for the following week.

Fluency Assessments for 1-6

Fluency Assessment

Description

The **Fluency Assessment** consists of passages and fluency record sheets to help you record oral reading accuracy and important aspects of oral reading fluency. The assessments will tell you how many words a student can read aloud per minute and how many of these words are read correctly. Information gathered from the Fluency Record Sheet may be used to verify or clarify instructional decisions. Oral Reading accuracy is a percentage score based on the total number of words read and the number of errors noted. The student should read 97% or more of the words correctly. When using the Oral Reading Fluency Norms chart, if a student's words correct per minute score falls more than ten points below the benchmarks shown, the student is not reading fluently.

How to administer

The Fluency Assessment is administered by asking a student to do a timed reading of a carefully selected grade-level passage. As the student reads, you follow along on a copy of the same text and record errors such as omissions, substitutions, mistakes, insertions of words or parts of words, and hesitations of more than three seconds. To calculate the number of words read correctly in one minute, subtract the number of errors from the total number of words read.

When to administer

The fluency passages serve two purposes. They can be administered three times a year as benchmark tests to determine if students are reading fluently. They can also be used every unit so that you can monitor progress and determine if students are meeting instructional goals. Record the information for each student on the Fluency Record Sheet for that passage.

Teacher Tips

Fluency assessments should be repeated periodically throughout the school year to monitor growth. Use at least two selections every two to three weeks for most students. In addition, provide frequent opportunities for fluency practice in between scheduled assessments.

Benchmark Books and Running Records for K-6

Running Records

Description

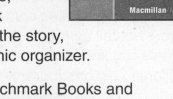

Running Records help teachers identify a student's reading level, style, and strategy use. They help determine a student's independent, instructional, and frustrational reading levels. You can also obtain an accuracy rate, error rate, and a self-correction rate. You can check the students' comprehension by having them retell the story, answer comprehension questions, or fill out a graphic organizer.

The Benchmark Levels of the Running Record Benchmark Books and passages align with the **Macmillan/McGraw-Hill Treasures** Leveled Readers, as well as DRA, Guided Reading, and Reading Recovery levels.

How to administer

There are thirty Benchmark Books for levels Rebus through twenty-eight, and sixteen passages in the teacher's manual for levels thirty through eighty. Each leveled text appears on the running record form to simplify the recording of miscues. Total the number of miscues and self-corrections, then calculate the reading accuracy and self-correction rates to determine the student's instructional level.

When to administer

Running records should be taken every three to four weeks to monitor progress and document the student's developing reading strategies.

Teacher Tips

Do not prompt the student in any way. If you need to say the word for the student, then score it as an error. Use both the fiction and nonfiction Benchmark Books and passages to determine reading levels.

Unit and Benchmark Assessments for K-6

Unit Assessment

Description

The **Unit Assessment** includes a fiction and a nonfiction passage, and questions focusing on the main skills taught throughout the unit. There is also a writing prompt which gives students an opportunity to practice writing in a test situation. The Unit Assessment is a formative assessment. Evaluate the results to diagnose students' strengths and weaknesses. Scores that fall below the 80th percentile suggest that students require additional instruction. The Teacher's Edition lists Additional Lessons for remediation.

Test Item Validation

The Unit Assessments contain validated test items. Validated test items are questions that are field tested to ensure their **reliability** and **validity**. A *valid* question accurately measures what it says it is supposed to measure. A *reliable* question is dependable, and provides the same results each time. Validated test items are subjected to a rigorous item development process. The statistical information about reliability and item difficulty are reviewed before questions are deemed acceptable.

How to administer

You may choose to give the Unit Assessment in one sitting or schedule the writing for another time. This assessment is not intended to be timed, but for planning purposes, it should take approximately one hour. Each Unit Assessment consists of twenty-eight multiple-choice questions, one short-response and one extended-response question, and a Writing Prompt.

When to administer

Administer the tests at the end of each unit.

> ### Teacher Tips
> When Unit Assessments are used for grading purposes, the tests can be considered **outcome** or *summative* assessments. Summative assessments summarize what students know, and are used for accountability.

Benchmark Assessment

Description

The **Benchmark Assessment** can be used to measure student progress throughout the year. There are two parallel forms of the test covering the same skills, and they are of equal difficulty. The scores on the Benchmark Assessment should improve over time. The first Benchmark Assessment is administered in the fall, and scores are likely to be low as the items represent skills that may not have been taught yet. Scores on the assessment administered mid-year should show an overall increase, and the scores at the end of the year should be the most improved of all. The Benchmark Assessments align with the standards and objectives of standardized tests, most notably the TerraNova 2nd Edition and the National Assessment of Educational Progress (NAEP). They also align with the instructional design and skills built into the Treasures program.

Test Item Validation

The Benchmark Assessments contain validated test items. (See page 18 for an explanation of validated test items.)

How to administer

You can administer the assessment in one or two sittings, or schedule the writing for another time. This assessment is not intended to be timed, but for planning purposes, should take approximately two hours. Each Benchmark Assessment consists of fifty-five multiple-choice questions, five short-response and two extended-response questions, and a Writing Prompt.

When to administer

Administer Form A of the test at the beginning of the year and at the end of the year. Administer Form B of the test in the middle of the year.

Teacher Tips

If you compare or graph the results, scores should show an increase for each student. Students who do not show an improvement in scores should be further evaluated for additional support or the Intervention Program. The Benchmark Assessment gives you advance warning for accountability tests. The test identifies which topic areas might benefit from further work before the actual state or standardized test is taken.

Alternative Assessments

ELL Practice and Assessment

Weekly Tests

Description

Each **Weekly Test** consists of vocabulary, phonics, comprehension and grammar questions. The format and length of the test varies, and requires students to circle the correct word, match items to the correct answer, or write an answer to a constructed-response question.

When to administer

Administer the test when you have completed the week of instruction. The test should take approximately twenty minutes to complete.

How to administer

Distribute copies of the test to each student. Be sure that all students understand the directions. Answer questions about procedures and materials, but do not assist students with answering test items.

Teacher Tips

Certain assessment accommodations will not affect the results of the test. Changes that do not change the task in a meaningful way, such as reading the directions aloud or using a place marker, are allowed. Other accommodations that are permitted include bilingual word lists and dictionaries, clarifications of directions, and directions that are translated into native languages.

Alternative Assessments

ELL Practice and Assessment

Unit Progress Tests

Description

The **Unit Progress Test** is a four-page assessment based on the unit's themes, strategies, and skills. There are multiple-choice, matching, and constructed-response questions that cover vocabulary, phonics, comprehension, grammar, and editing. Students will also complete a graphic organizer, and read and edit a proofreading passage.

How to administer

Distribute copies of the test to each student. Monitor students' test-taking behavior to make sure that each student is following the directions and writing responses in the correct places.

When to administer

Administer the test at the end of the unit. The test should take approximately forty minutes to complete.

Teacher Tips

The **ELL Practice and Assessment** book includes additional **Study Guide** pages preceding every Unit Progress Test. Use the Study Guide pages before students take the actual tests for additional review and practice of the skills that are assessed on the test.

Recording Forms

ELL Practice and Assessment

Yearly Language Record

- Use the Language Development Record form to record the results of the weekly comprehension checks.
- Student responses should be indicated as beginning, intermediate, or advanced.
- In addition, note any additional comments or observations you may have on the bottom of the form.
- Evaluate students' progress through the different language proficiency levels when doing your instructional planning and making grouping decisions.

Student Profiles

- Record observations, students' strengths and weaknesses, and test score results.
- Student Profile forms are provided for Language Development, Strategy and Skill Assessment, and Writing.

Writing Rubric

- Use the Writing Rubric to score students' writing in the areas of ideas and content, organization, voice, word choice, sentence fluency, and conventions. The rubric incorporates the skills needed to assess a variety of writing styles and methods.

Book Talks Forms

- Students can participate in Book Talks and record what they have learned by using the fiction and nonfiction Book Talks forms.

Peer Assessment Form

- Students can assess classmates' Book Talk presentations by recording what they liked best about the presentation and how their classmate can improve.

Self Assessment Form

- Students can assess their own progress by identifying their strengths and weaknesses, listing the new words they have learned, and formulating a plan for improvement.

Computer-Based Assessments

Test Generator

Use the **Test Generator** online or use the CD-ROM for electronic versions of the following assessments:

- **Weekly Assessment, Leveled Weekly Assessment**, and **ELL Weekly Test**
- **Unit Assessment** and **ELL Unit Progress Test**
- **Benchmark Assessment**

How to Use the Test Generator

- Score assessments online.

- View test reports for individual students or the whole class by specific skill and standard.

- Use reports to plan whole class and differentiated instruction.

- Access reteach and remediation suggestions for each assessed skill for students who need additional support.

- Build your own assessments with the Test Generator item bank

- Create a unit pretest for students with the Test Generator item bank:

1) Use the same blueprint (the same *number* of items and the same *kinds* of items) as the Unit Assessment.

2) Pretest scores should not count in a student's grade, because they have not had the opportunity to learn the material yet. Use them to highlight areas that students need to work on during the unit.

3) You can use pretests to organize flexible work groups around complementary skills.

- Administer a self-assessment.

1) An electronic pretest is a way for students to do a self-assessment. They can use their scores to help them focus on specific areas during the unit.

2) After the unit is over, if you have constructed parallel pretests and unit tests, students can make a bar or line graph of "before" and "after" scores.

Writing Assessments

Weekly Writing in the Teacher's Edition

Description

- Each week students practice writing in a different mode. They model their own writing after a student writing sample, and learn how to edit and revise their work by using the writing process.

- Students write about something related to the theme or concept for the week.

- The weekly writing prepares students for the Unit Writing Workshop at the end of each unit. The weekly writing lessons build throughout the unit as students develop the skills needed for each specific mode of writing. The five weeks of writing culminate in a unit-level writing process workshop.

How to Use for Assessment

- Holistic scoring rubrics are provided to score the weekly writing. The rubrics are based on the six-trait writing model for assessing writing.

- Each week students focus on a particular writing trait, such as ideas and content, organization, voice, word choice, sentence fluency, or conventions. This helps teach them how to improve their writing and raise their writing scores.

- Practice in writing prepares students for standardized writing tests and holistic scoring.

Writing Assessments

Unit Writing Workshop in the Teacher's Edition

Description

- The **Unit Writing Workshop** focuses on the skills needed to produce a finished piece of writing. Each unit covers a particular mode of writing.

- The workshop instructs students in how to plan and organize their writing, write and revise a draft, and finally proofread and publish a finished piece of writing.

- Test-strategy lessons show students how to evaluate a writing sample and revise and edit. This gives students the skills to edit their own writing.

How to Use for Assessment

- Student writing is scored with a six-traits writing rubric. There are four-point and six-point Scoring Rubrics to use for assessing students' writing.

- Students can participate by assessing their own work. They can use a Writer's Checklist to help them improve their writing and be sure that all six writing traits are fully developed.

- **Anchor Papers** in the back of the **Unit and Benchmark Assessment** book provide samples of student writing for each score point on the four-point writing rubric. Under each sample is an explanation of how the writing measures up to each of the six writing traits. Use these samples to provide a baseline for comparison when you are grading actual student papers.

Assessment Timetable

Assessment / Purpose (s)	Times (s)
TPRI (K-3), DIBELS (K-3), Fox in a Box (K-2) Screening, Diagnostic, and Progress Monitoring	Screen three times a year: Students who don't pass the screen, monitor up to once per unit until readiness is reached
Screening, Diagnostic, Placement Assessment Screening, Diagnostic, and Placement	Screening and Placement at start of year Re-administer to diagnose as needed
Informal Observations Progress Monitoring	Daily; ongoing
Fluency Assessments Progress Monitoring	One group per week: approaching level students every two weeks; on level every three weeks; beyond level every six weeks
Running Records Progress Monitoring	Every three to four weeks
Weekly Assessment Progress Monitoring	Weekly
Unit Assessment Progress Monitoring; Outcome	End of Unit (about every six weeks)
Benchmark Assessment Progress Monitoring	Three times a year: Fall, Winter, Spring

Building Portfolios

Portfolio Assessments

A portfolio is a collection of student work organized for a particular purpose.

- Portfolios are used to show development and show best work.

- A portfolio that shows development contains examples of the writing process and samples from the beginning, middle, and end of the year.

- Portfolios that are filled with the student's best work are used primarily for showcasing what the student has learned. For example, this kind of portfolio may be on display when parents visit the school for an "open school night."

- Portfolios can be used to connect students' learning from unit to unit. Students are asked to choose certain pieces of work from the previous unit, and then reflect on them. This reflection can take the form of a note attached to the work, or a more formal journal-style entry.

- A Reflection Form can be used to help students describe what they have learned. Students need to learn that it is not necessary to reflect upon an entire lesson or activity. For example, a student might write, "I learned that *baseball* is a compound word. Baseball is my favorite sport." The student might illustrate this with a drawing of a bat and ball. These kinds of connections are important to help students internalize what they are learning. See page 30 for a sample Reflection Form.

The charts that follow outline a portfolio development process (page 28), and demonstrate two different applications: a developmental portfolio and a best work portfolio (page 29). On page 31 is a Portfolio Rubric to use when evaluating students' portfolios.

Portfolio Planning Process

1 **Set a purpose.** Decide what information you need, and how you and your students will use it. Let that decision drive the rest of your portfolio planning.

2 **Define role of student.** At minimum, students should reflect on the work in their portfolios. Should they help choose some of the contents? Help evaluate? Have a rationale for this that matches your purpose.

3 **Identify other users and uses.** Who, besides you and the student, will see the portfolios, and why? Parents? Peers (during pair or group instruction, for example)?

4 **Identify elements of portfolio.** What work should go into the portfolio? Will you specify each work, or will you let students choose? Perhaps a combination of both? How will student reflections be collected?

5 **Plan a process for construction and review.** How will the work be identified? How many samples do you need? What sort of container (folder, bin, file) will you use? Will computer files, audiotapes, and other non-paper pieces of evidence be allowed? When will there be time for students to systematically review and reflect upon their work?

6 **Gather evidence.** According to your plan, have students fill their portfolio with work samples. This is usually done as a part of a regular lesson time.

7 **Interpret evidence.** Allow students to help you understand what their work means. Use student reflection sheets, or sticky-notes, or some way of recording their reflections. You can use the portfolios as material for teacher-student conferences, too.

8 **Use materials for instructional and/or evaluation decisions.** Repeat steps 6 and 7 until the purpose has been served.

Portfolio Planning Process

Two Examples of the Portfolio Planning Process

STEP IN THE PROCESS	EXAMPLE 1 A Developmental Portfolio	EXAMPLE 2 A Best Work Portfolio
1. Set Purpose	The student will keep a personal reading portfolio to provide **formative** information to support progress as a reader.	The student will keep a best work reading portfolio to provide **summative** information as evidence for progress as a reader.
2. Define Role of Student	The student decides what to include based on a rubric. Student reflections on reading and what needs improvement will be the primary information.	The student and the teacher choose the work based on a rubric. The work is used for grading. Student reflections on reading focus on accomplishments.
3. Identify Other Users and Uses	The teacher will use the evidence in the portfolio for reading conferences with the students. The portfolios will not be used for grading.	The teacher may use the evidence in the portfolio for reading conferences with students or parents, and for grading.
4. Define Elements of Portfolio	The student completes a reflection form for the contents of the portfolio as a whole.	The work is chosen by the teacher and student. Student reflects on each piece to explain the choice.
5. Plan Construction and Review Process	Explain purpose to students. Make folders. Have a lesson(s) about how to write good reflections. Schedule conferences with students, and allow time for them to prepare their reflections.	Explain purpose to students. Make folders. Share the rules for selection of work. Have a lesson(s) about how to write good reflections. Explain the criteria to be used for grading.
6. Gather Evidence	Students work on portfolios.	Students work on portfolios.
7. Interpret Evidence	At conferences, the teacher asks the student to share reflections and what the student has learned.	The teacher, and perhaps the student as well, applies the rubric to the portfolio contents.
8. Use for Decisions	The primary decisions are instructional.	The primary decisions are accountability and outcome decisions.

Name _____ Date _____

Reading Portfolio Reflections

I chose this piece of work for my portfolio (name it):

This piece shows that I can (or that I have learned)...
(List as many things as you can here, and tell why)

This piece shows that I still need to work on...

Here's how I plan to do that:

Name _____ Date _____

Reading Portfolio Rubric		
Score	**Criteria**	**Comments**
4	All required pieces are included. Each piece has a thoughtful reflection sheet. Pieces show student does high quality work and understands why it is high quality work.	
3	All required pieces are included. Each piece has a reflection sheet; most are thoughtful. Pieces show student does good work and understands why it is good work.	
2	All required pieces are included. Most pieces have a completed reflection sheet. Pieces show student has met most of the learning targets for the period.	
1	Some required pieces are missing. Some pieces have a completed reflection sheet. Pieces are at a minimally acceptable level.	
0	Some required pieces are missing. Few pieces have a completed reflection sheet. Pieces show student has not met learning targets for the period.	

Using Multiple Measures

The Assessment Process

The assessment process is making instructional decisions based on assessment information.

- All decisions should be based on "multiple measures" or more than one kind of assessment or set of scores.

- The process starts with collecting assessment evidence (test results, observations).

- The next step is to compare and interpret the information you have gathered.

- The third step is to make instructional decisions based on your conclusions.

- This process is ongoing: collect evidence, interpret, make decisions...

The Assessment Process

Collect and review **Assessment Evidence.**
Use multiple sources of evidence (test scores, observations).

Decide what the evidence **Means.**
Compare and contrast scores and observations with other assessment results.

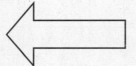

Make **Instructional Decisions** based on the conclusions you have drawn.

Using Multiple Measures

Managing the Information

There are times when a set of results about one student will not be consistent. This is more likely to be the case for younger students, but it can happen at any grade. For example, a first-grade student may have IRI results that suggest he does not recognize common sight words, but your Fluency results may suggest that he does. Which is correct?

- In this case, start with the working hypothesis that the student does recognize these words. Place him in a small group and continue to monitor his progress with additional fluency assessments to make sure your hypothesis was correct. If it wasn't, change his placement and his instruction.

- For instructional decisions, use a variety of assessments to make judgments. Look at additional test results to get a better idea of how the student is progressing.

- In addition, the IRI (and fluency assessments or running records) can be repeated to make sure that this decision about the student is accurate.

Organizing Information at the Start of the Year

You may wish to use the forms on the following pages to record scores and organize your screening, diagnostic, and placement information at the beginning of the year.

- Three versions of the Primary Grades form are provided, depending on whether you used the TPRI, DIBELS, or the Placement Test for the initial screening or placement decisions.

- Enter results or scores on the chart, and check off the appropriate instructional levels.

- Draw conclusions based on your data and use the information to plan your instruction.

Primary Grades
Screening/Diagnostic Information For Starting The Year

Name	TPRI*							IRI**			RR**		
	G K	P A	W R	F	L C	R A	R C	IND	INS	FR	IND	INS	FR

* **TPRI Scales:** Graphophonemic Knowledge (GK), Phonemic Awareness (PA), Word Reading (WR), Fluency (F), Listening Comprehension (LC), Reading Accuracy (RA), Reading Comprehension (RC): √ = Developed; - = Still Developing
** **IRI, RR Levels:** Independent (IND), Instructional (INS), Frustrational (FR)

Primary Grades
Screening/Diagnostic Information For Starting The Year

Name	DIBELS*					IRI**			RR**		
	ISF	PSF	NWF	LNF	ORF	IND	INS	FR	IND	INS	FR

* **DIBELS Scales:** Initial Sound Fluency (ISF), Phoneme Segmentation Fluency (PSF), Nonsense Word Fluency (NWF), Letter Naming Fluency (LNF), Oral Reading Fluency (ORF): √ = Low risk; - = Some risk; X = At risk
** **IRI, RR Levels:** Independent (IND), Instructional (INS), Frustrational (FR)

Primary Grades
Diagnostic/Placement Information For Starting The Year

Name	Placement Test*				IRI**			RR**		
	PH	WR	VOC	RC	IND	INS	FR	IND	INS	FR

* **Placement Scores:** Phonics (PH), Word Recognition (WR), Vocabulary (VOC), Reading Comprehension (RC)
** **IRI, RR Levels:** Independent (IND), Instructional (INS), Frustrational (FR)

Name	Oral Reading Fluency*	Placement Test**		IRI***			RR***		
	WCPM	VOC	RC	IND	INS	FR	IND	INS	FR

Intermediate Grades
Screening/Diagnostic/Placement Information For Starting The Year

* **ORF:** Words connect per minute (WCPM); ** **Placement Tests:** Vocabulary (VOC), Reading Comprehension (RC);
*** **IRI, RR Levels:** Independent (IND), Instructional (INS), Frustrational (FR)

Forming Groups

Teacher-Led Small Groups

Data from assessments should be used to inform and modify instruction to meet student's needs. Working in teacher-led small groups allows you to address specific skills areas in which students need additional instruction, practice, reinforcement or extension. It is important to use both informal and formal assessments on an ongoing basis, and to keep in mind that students should not be in a particular group each time. Rather, a student will move to different groups based on his or her instructional needs.

- At the beginning of the year, results of screening, diagnostic, and placement assessments will give you information on what students' instructional needs are.

- As your students progress through the year, use the daily Quick Checks and observational assessments that are found in the Teacher's Edition.

- Weekly Assessments and Unit Assessments will also provide data on what to teach in small groups, and which students to address in those groups.

GROUPING OPTIONS	
Type of Group	**Major Uses**
Whole Group	Introduce, model, teach, and review key grade-level strategies, skills and concepts.
Small Groups	Provide additional instruction, practice, review, or extension on key strategies, skills, and concepts, based on common needs of students in a small group. Read leveled reading materials to apply key strategies, skills, and concepts.

Forming Groups

Guidelines for Working in Small Groups

Within the course of instruction, it is important that students engage in both homogeneous and heterogeneous groupings.

- Homogeneous means all of the students in the group have common instructional needs.

- Heterogeneous means the students have mixed abilities, and interact and learn from their peers.

- Use flexible groupings, based on need, for specific skill instruction that changes more frequently.

- Heterogeneous Groups can be used for Workstation activities.

- Consider additional observational information about students' instructional needs, work habits, and interpersonal skills when forming groups. For example, you may find that you have enough students reading on grade level to make two "on level" groups. Observations can help you include some "leaders" in each group. Avoid placing children together who do not get along, and allow you to mix assertive and quiet children in each group.

Assessment Opportunities

Informal Assessments

The reading classroom is full of assessment opportunities. Chances are you use some of them without realizing you are doing "assessment." Remember the definition of assessment is systematically gathering information about what students know and can do. In reading, you can do this in an informal way throughout instruction.

- **Teaching children to monitor their own comprehension:** Monitoring comprehension is an important comprehension strategy explicitly taught in **TREASURES** from grades one through six. Students can ask themselves questions about what they have just read. Good readers learn to use these metacognitive skills unconsciously. Have you ever said to yourself, "I am not sure what I just read"? Your automatic monitoring system helps you improve your comprehension of the text.

- **Ask students to retell** or explain in their own words what they have just read. A good explanation shows you what a student understands, and a poor explanation makes the student's misconceptions and misunderstandings apparent so you can address them.

- **Teach students how to monitor their own progress.** If children realize they do not understand something they have read, they can try various reading strategies and/or ask for help from peers or from their teacher. Listen for the substance of the answer, and not merely if it is "correct" or not. Learn from the student's answer what he or she is thinking.

Assessment Opportunities

Informal Assessments

Quick Checks: TREASURES provides many opportunities for you to observe students independently practice a strategy or skill taught in whole-group instruction. (See the Quick Checks Observation Forms on pages 42 and 43.)

- The Quick Check reminds you to observe your students and see if any of them are having difficulty with a skill they have just learned.

- You can use this information to decide if this is a skill you need to address in small-group instruction.

Assignments: Every assignment or activity allows you to assess reading behaviors. Assignments do not need to be formally graded, but they should be treated as a potential source of information about what students know, what they still need to learn, and what their misconceptions or difficulties are.

- Review assignments, noting both strengths and weaknesses, and present the student with oral or written feedback.

- Ask students to go over their own assignments in groups, where peers can point out their strengths and weaknesses to each other. Note that this is an opportunity to show students that looking at what is right and wrong is important.

- Ask students to go over their own work and reflect upon it. This, too, is a skill that needs to be modeled and taught.

Classroom Observations: You have opportunities to observe your students at work and at play, working alone, and interacting with other students. Be systematic with the way you do and record the observations.

- Does this child like to read or look at books? What topics is she interested in?

- How does this child work with others?

- You can ask students what kinds of stories or books they like. You should strive to create a print-rich environment, with materials at a wide range of reading levels on as many topics as possible. Expand on students' interests and introduce new ones.

QUICK CHECKS OBSERVATIONS FORM (PRIMARY)

Student's Name	Phonemic Awareness	Phonics	Fluency	Comprehension	Vocabulary

QUICK CHECKS OBSERVATIONS FORM (INTERMEDIATE)				
Student's Name	**Phonics**	**Fluency**	**Comprehension**	**Vocabulary**

Assessment Opportunities

Feedback IS Assessment

Using corrective feedback as an assessment tool: Feedback should help students see how they can improve their work. The most useful feedback is a specific comment describing the strengths and weaknesses of individual work, with useful suggestions for improvement. To be useful and motivating, feedback needs to be...

- Delivered in the form of praise

- Modeled for the student

- Practiced by the student

- Used continually over time

Feedback can be oral or written: Feedback needs to be immediate. Correct students' errors as soon as they occur.

- Give feedback orally for younger students and non-readers.

- For older students and good readers, writing positive feedback on their work is helpful. Written comments are more lasting; students can refer back to them.

Asking for feedback: Encourage students to ask for feedback or help when they need it. It is important for students to learn to monitor their own work.

- You can have students place green (I'm OK) and red (I need help) circles or traffic lights on their desk to let you know they need help without disrupting others. Or you can use smiley-faces and frowning-faces for this same purpose.

- This allows you to give feedback and assistance in a timely fashion so that students do not lose momentum or miss something because they were stuck.

- If you use a system like this, the oral feedback you give in response to these requests should follow the same feedback principles. Don't just give "answers." Give feedback that will help the student learn from the mistakes.

How to give good feedback: The table on page 45 models some ways for you to provide corrective feedback to your students.

How To Give Corrective Feedback

FEEDBACK SHOULD BE...	HOW TO MODEL IT	EXAMPLES
Delivered in the form of praise	Direct your comment at some aspect of the work, not the student. Use descriptive adjectives. Avoid judgmental words. Make I-statements not You-statements.	*DON'T SAY:* "You need to write more about the main character." *SAY:* "The main character was interesting. I want to know more about him." *DON'T SAY:* "Good job!" *SAY:* "Your story makes me want to meet your pet!"
Modeled for the student	Refer to specific aspects of the work. Be specific, not general	*DON'T SAY:* "The story summary was poor." *SAY:* "The story held my interest. It would be a better story if there were more details."
Practiced by the student	Allow the student to have a turn giving himself feedback.	*DON'T SAY:* "This isn't clear." *SAY:* "You try it now. What suggestion can you make to improve this essay?"
Used continually over time	Provide opportunities for the student to practice giving himself feedback.	*DON'T SAY:* "Tell me what is wrong with your story." *HAVE THE STUDENT RESPOND:* "My story needs a stronger ending."

How to Make Instructional Decisions

What to Do to Make Decisions

To make sound instructional decisions, you should do the following:

- **Interpret:** "This means that he is comprehending beyond grade level because he is good at using context clues. He figures out what the words mean so fast that he skips over some vocabulary and doesn't learn it."

- **Decide:** What can you do to meet the student's learning needs.

- **Check:** As you collect ongoing information about student progress, continue to check this information against your interpretation or hypothesis.

- **Modify** your instructional decisions if they are not achieving the intended results.

Compare results from different assessments:

- Look for corroborating evidence across the different kinds of assessments; use multiple measures.

- Different sources of information should reinforce your decisions.

The types of instructional decisions you need to make include the following:

- Decisions about grouping (who to teach).

- Decisions about learning goals and objectives (what to teach).

- Decisions about materials, methods, and rate of instruction (how to teach).

HOW TO MAKE INSTRUCTIONAL DECISIONS

GROUPING

- Will I use small groups? How many do I need?
- How will I decide which student is in which group?
- How will I handle independent work?
- How will I handle whole-class instruction?
- How will I set up the workstations?

LEARNING GOALS OR OBJECTIVES

- Which goals or objectives will I emphasize? Review? Reteach?
- Which goals or objectives will require less emphasis?
- In what order will I teach them?

MATERIALS

- Which grade-level materials should be used in reading instruction?
- Which grade-level materials should be available for independent (recreational) reading?
- What topics or kinds of stories would most interest the students?

METHODS

- Which techniques or approaches should I use in lessons?
- Which techniques are best suited for the learning objectives I need to emphasize?
- Which techniques involve students in the learning the most?

RATE OF INSTRUCTION

- How much time should be allotted to each lesson?
- How fast or slow should students be asked to move through particular material?
- What might need to be reviewed several times (take up several lessons) and what might be touched on more lightly?

Making Instructional Decisions

How to Apply Your Decisions

Adjusting Lesson Plans

- Students are achieving the learning targets you set for them, so continue with the next step in the materials, according to your district curriculum.

- Areas of strength are identified, so plan enrichment lessons or activities.

- Areas of difficulty are identified, so plan reteaching lessons.

Identifying Learning Targets

Learning targets for review or remediation should come directly from the assessment information. Share this information with the students so that they understand what their goals and objectives are.

REVIEW or RETEACH?

REVIEW

- For minor difficulties, continue with instruction as planned and incorporate review into seatwork, workstations, or small group instruction.

- Reinforce those concepts during regular instruction, focusing attention on the concept by oral questioning and discussion.

- Example: Students had some difficulty with comma use in the last unit. Proceed to the next unit but incorporate extra practice with commas into daily work and also explicitly point out comma usage in the next stories or text students read.

RETEACH

- Reteach concepts that were difficult for the whole class or for specific groups of students.

- Reteach all or part of a unit by using a mixture of old and new materials. Students can profit from correcting work they have already done and explaining the reasons for the corrections, either orally to you or other students or in writing.

- **Treasures** provides instructional materials at the approaching level for reteaching, as well as Additional Lessons in the Teacher's Editions.

Making Instructional Decisions

Modifying Instruction

Changing the Mode of Instruction

- Vary the way you present the skills and concepts.

- Change the kind of student engagement or response required.

- Increase student practice in addition to reteaching the concept.

Choosing Materials

Appropriate materials for reviewing and reteaching are listed in the Teacher's Edition. You can also use leveled books, trade books, writing resources, practice workbooks, and any other materials that match the learning objectives.

> **VARY methods for reviewing or reteaching.**
> **Don't repeat what didn't work before!**

You can use some of the same materials, but in a different way.

- For example, if a student did not do well on a test or assignment, have her go back over it (individually or with a peer tutor or in a small group that does this with each of the members) and say or write *why* the correct answer is correct.

- Do this in a positive manner, giving reasons why an answer is or is not correct.

- If a student can put things in her own words, she is much more likely to "understand" it.

Use new or different materials and vary the teaching method.

- For example, if using flash cards didn't work the first time for learning a set of vocabulary words, try something else like writing the words in sentences.

- Use more active methods with objectives students find difficult.

- Use several methods for difficult objectives.

- Give more individual feedback in these targeted review areas.

- Allow for student practice, self-assessment, and use of feedback.

To reteach, don't use the same instructional strategy. Use one of the several instructional strategies provided in the Teacher's Edition.

Making Instructional Decisions

Modifying Instruction

Look for Patterns in Assessment Results

Sometimes there will be a clear group pattern in the test results.

- Look for a small group of students who missed the same skill or objective.

- Form a group based on this information, and reteach those skills.

Fluency Opportunities

Students whose fluency is below expectations need extra opportunities to practice.

- Additional fluency activities are available in the Fluency Solutions CDs and in the Additional Lessons provided with this series.

- Reading aloud is a motivating way for students to work together. More experienced peers can "coach" their classmates as they listen to them read.

- More experienced peers can get good experience by reading stories aloud to classmates that the less fluent readers would not be able to read themselves.

- Monitor these groups closely, and circulate and assist as needed. Peer tutoring does not work well if the peers act as "substitute teachers." The teacher needs to remain in the role of supervisor.

Formative Assessment in Fluency Includes Self-Assessment

- Students can use a tape recorder to listen to themselves, and then they can discuss with you what they heard.

- Students may "hear" hesitations or mispronunciations, but they do not know what to do about them. Provide help one-on-one or in small group discussions.

Using the Weekly and Unit Evaluation Sheets

The evaluations sheets that follow each weekly and unit test tell you the specific skills that need to be reviewed or retaught. Compare these results with your own observations.

- Identify one or more objectives from the week or unit that need reinforcement. Add them to your lesson objectives for the next week for one student, for a group of students, or for the whole class, whichever is indicated.

- Decide how you will work these objectives into individual, group, or whole-class work so that the students who need practice get it.

WAYS TO ADDRESS WEAKNESSES

- Reteach skills that a significant number of students are weak in.

- Use appropriate assignments (see "Diagnose and Prescribe" Charts in Teachers' Guides) as seatwork and center work during the next unit.

- Form groups for peer tutoring by using one student's strength to assist with another student's weakness. Mix groups often and don't allow one student to always be the "weak" one.

- Use targeted review games as activities.

- Use individual student work as the basis for student conferences. Plan with the student what he or she needs to work on, and how that can be done.

WAYS TO BUILD ON STRENGTHS

- Extend the unit if a significant number of students are strong in the same area. For example, have students read a similar story in one of the leveled texts.

- Add assignments that allow students to excel at something they are good at as seatwork or center work during the next unit.

- Form groups for peer tutoring by using one student's strength to assist with another student's weakness. Mix groups often and don't allow one student to always be the "weak" one.

- Have students make up games or activities that others can play.

- Use individual student work as the basis for student conferences. Help the student explain what exactly the strength is, and plan with the student what he or she will do next as a result.

WAYS TO KEEP INSTRUCTION "ON TRACK"

- Continue with the next unit when possible – incorporating reteaching or extension work as necessary into ongoing progress.

- Keep concepts and skills from previous units of instruction "at the ready" by using games, activities, and seatwork that incorporate systematic review.

- Ask students to identify previous concepts, skills, or reading strategies as they use them (that is, make sure students are aware of what they know).

- Use portfolios or other methods for student self-reflection for reviewing concepts and building a skill repertoire.

Making Instructional Decisions

Case Studies

Instructional decisions need to be set in the context of what will work for all students in your classroom. It's a balancing act. The case studies that follow describe some of the assessment information you will be using to make instructional decisions. They also show you how the assessments for Screening, Diagnosis, Placement, and Progress Monitoring work together.

Case Study, Grade 1

Starting the School Year

During these first days of school, Ms. Wooten is **making observations** about her class that will be relevant for all the subjects she is to teach.

- She observes student behavior, attitudes, and interests.

- She collects screening, diagnostic, and placement information for her students.

- She uses the **Screening, Diagnostic, Placement Assessment** book, and administers the TPRI for screening, and the Informal Reading Inventory and Running Records for diagnostic and placement information.

The chart on page 53 summarizes this information for her 20 students. Notice that the class includes a wide range of student **reading readiness**.

- Some students have not passed through the TPRI screening. As developing readers, they are not administered an IRI.

- Others are at various levels in first grade materials and she takes Running Records on these students as well as an IRI.

- A few students are already reading on the second grade level and they take an IRI and a Running Record as well.

On the basis of this **screening and diagnostic information**, Ms. Wooten makes several instructional decisions.

- First, she establishes reading groups. She sees them as tentative and will continue to monitor progress. Students who are doing well will be moved.

Case Study - Ms. Wooten's First Grade Class
Screening/Diagnostic Information For Starting The Year

Name	TPRI*							IRI**	RR**
	GK	PA	WR	F	LC	RA	RC	IRI- Inst. Level	
Asher, Lee	√	√	√	–	√	√	–	(no IRI given)	1
Beihler, Sam	(passed screening)							1	12
Bickman, Sarah	√	–	–	–	√	–	–	(no IRI given)	R
Brown, Jamal	(passed screening)							1	12
Dreeben, Emily	(passed screening)							2	18
Duncan, Kara	(passed screening)							1	10
Fish, Trevor	(passed screening)							1	12
Frees, Charity	√	–	–	–	–	–	–	(no IRI given)	R
Ghee, Mai	(passed screening)							1	12
Hanson, Harlen	√	√	√	√	√	√	–	(no IRI given)	3
Hill, LaShaunda	√	√	–	√	√	√	√	(no IRI given)	2
Juarez, Juan	√	√	√	–	√	√	√	(no IRI given)	2
Kanter, Horace	√	√	√	–	√	√	√	(no IRI given)	2
Morris, Kate	(passed screening)							1	12
Murphy, Tom	√	–	–	–	√	–	–	(no IRI given)	R
Nicely, John	√	–	–	–	√	–	–	(no IRI given)	R
Platt, Mina	(passed screening)							2	18
Powell, Devon	(passed screening)							2	18
Singer, Sue	√	√	√	–	√	√	√	(no IRI given)	2
Solomon, Carrie	√	√	–	√	√	√	√	(no IRI given)	2

* **TPRI Scales:** Graphophonemic Knowledge (GK), Phonemic Awareness (PA), Word Reading (WR), Fluency (F), Listening Comprehension (LC), Reading Accuracy (RA), Reading Comprehension (RC): √ = Developed; - = Developing
** **IRI, RR Levels:** Independent (IND), Instructional (INS), Frustrational (FR)

Making Instructional Decisions

Case Study, Grade 1 (continued)

The second thing Ms. Wooten does is decide on a selection of materials.

- Approaching level (Benchmark Level Rebus), on level (Benchmark Levels 3-16), or beyond level (Benchmark Levels 18 or above).

- She will begin instruction with the indicated materials and adjust the materials as she monitors student progress.

- TPRI results suggest that she should emphasize Phonemic Awareness for the pre-reading group (Group A). Note that students who were not given an IRI did not place high enough in the Word List to be able to read grade-level text. Students who passed the screener and only missed one or two tests are on level.

Here are her initial reading groups:

Ms. Wooten's Initial Reading Groups			
Group A Working on readiness, Using pre-reading materials	**Group B** Working at beginning first grade level; using some on level and some approaching level materials	**Group C** Working at mid-first grade level; using on level materials and some beyond level materials	**Group D** Working at second grade level; using on level (2nd grade) materials and some beyond level materials
Sarah Bickman Charity Frees Tom Murphy John Nicely	Lee Asher Harlen Hanson LaShaunda Hill Juan Juarez Horace Kanter Sue Singer Carrie Solomon	Sam Beihler Jamal Brown Kara Duncan Trevor Fish Mai Ghee Kate Morris	Emily Dreeben Mina Platt Devon Powell

Making Instructional Decisions

Case Study, Grade 1 (continued)

The third thing Ms. Wooten decides is where to target some extra help. In particular, it looks like fluency is an issue, not only for the pre-readers but also for a group of the students in Group B: Lee Asher, Juan Juarez, Horace Kanter, and Sue Singer.

- She decides to emphasize fluency-building activities.

- She will read to students every day, selecting books based on student interests. She will do this as a whole class activity.

- She will include a listening station at the back of the classroom, and cycle the eight students from Groups A and B who need help with fluency (Bickman, Frees, Murphy, Nicely, Asher, Juarez, Kanter, and Singer) through it during individual work time.

- She will use the Fluency CDs as the main instructional materials here, and will also allow students to bring recordings of stories and songs to share on designated days.

- She will have an instructional session first, so students know how to use the station. There are three other centers, too, and they will change from time to time. The Teachers Guides have suggestions for learning centers.

Ms. Wooten has noted the Independent and Frustrational reading levels of each reader based on the IRIs.

- Students in Groups A and B can look at picture books independently.

- Students in Group C can read beginning first grade books independently.

- Students in Group D can read all first grade materials independently.

- This means that Ms. Wooten needs to give directions for any whole-class assignment out loud, at least for now.

- Any written directions for a whole-class assignment should be at a beginning first grade level and be read aloud.

- Directions for each reading group's particular work will be adjusted accordingly; for example, Group D should be able to read and follow directions written at an ending first-grade level.

Making Instructional Decisions

Case Study, Grade 1 (continued)

Progress Monitoring with Ongoing Informal and Formal Assessments

After the groups have been formed, Ms. Wooten handles Reading and Language Arts instruction with a mixture of **whole-class and small-group instruction**.

- Some phonics, fluency and comprehension activities are done in a whole-class setting in addition to reading.

- Ms. Wooten tries to spend 15 minutes a day with each small group, during which time she has assigned both individual seatwork and center work (two or three students at a time at one of the four learning centers in the back of the classroom).

- The children also know that if they finish their assigned work before time is called they may read (or look at) any book at their desk, or practice writing or math.

Ongoing assessments are needed to monitor progress on the specific knowledge and skills that form the learning objectives.

- Formal assessments, in the form of Weekly and Unit tests, serve this purpose for the whole class and for reading group objectives.

- Ms. Wooten keeps the results of these assessments at two levels. At the individual level, she records the grades in her grade book, and keeps the test Evaluation Sheets in student folders. At the class level, she uses the skills identified as strengths and weaknesses for ongoing instructional decisions, mostly about what objectives to emphasize or re-emphasize during reading groups or center work.

- For example, after each Weekly Test, she selects additional practice materials in the weakest skills for both seatwork and for one of the centers.

Monitoring progress also refers to the overall reading goal that students will improve in fluency, vocabulary, and comprehension, at increasing levels of text.

- For Groups A and B, Ms. Wooten administers a Fluency Assessment or a Running Record every other week.

- She does a Fluency Assessment or a Running Record about every third week for the students in Group C.

- She does a Fluency Assessment or a Running Record about once a month for the students in Group D.

- She keeps these records in a folder for each student.

Making Instructional Decisions

Case Study, Grade 1 (continued)

Outcome Assessment

Progress monitoring has allowed Ms. Wooten to "keep tabs" on her students' progress, individually and as a group.

- At the end of each unit, and at the end of each marking period, (these are not always at the same time in her school district), she also needs outcome measures.

- The Unit Tests give outcome information about learning goals for the unit. These are useful for future instructional decisions, but they also help her evaluate how successful she thinks her teaching of the unit has been.

For report card grades, Ms. Wooten will consider information from several sources.

- The district has a special first grade report card that includes sub-categories under Reading and Language Arts. The first grade report cards use a coding system, not A-F letters: Developing, Proficient, and Advanced. She assembles a set of evidence for each grade (D, P, or A) she must give.

- For example, under "Comprehension" she looks at evidence from the comprehension section of the unit test, from several comprehension assignments, and from her assessment of students' reading and discussion during reading group. Each of these is documented (in her grade book) and could be shown to parents if they asked about grades.

- Because the coding categories on the first grade report card are like levels on a rubric, she doesn't "average" the scores. Her assessment results are not all on the same scale anyway, so averaging doesn't make sense. Rather, she makes a judgment about the set of evidence, using the reporting codes as a rubric.

Making Instructional Decisions
Case Studies
Case Study, Grade 5
Starting the School Year

During these first days, Mr. Phelps is making observations about his class that will be relevant for all the subjects he is to teach.

- The students are given their first "no-grade" writing assignment. They read their stories aloud to the class, one a day, during the month of September. This gives students an authentic audience for their writing and some fluency practice.

- Mr. Phelps is making observations about student behavior, attitudes, and interests.

- He uses the **Screening, Diagnostic, Placement Assessment** book to find out initial instructional reading levels, and areas of individual and class strengths and weaknesses. His students represent a range of reading levels and interests. One student, Kevin Nunez, is an English Language Learner who would have found the fifth grade placement test too frustrating. Kevin moved into the school's area in the middle of fourth grade, and the decision not to administer the fifth grade placement test was based on his fourth grade records.

Look at the chart on page 59 for some of the results from the **diagnostic and placement assessments**.

On the basis of this screening and diagnostic information, Mr. Phelps makes several instructional decisions.

- First, he establishes reading groups.

- He sees them as tentative and will continue to monitor progress.

- Students who are doing well will be moved.

Case Study - Mr. Phelps's Fifth Grade Class
Diagnostic and Placement Information For Starting The Year

Name	Placement		IRI Comprehension Levels		
	Vocabulary	Comprehension	Independent	Instructional	Frustrational
Abel, Larry	85	83	4	5	6
Benz, Carol	80	80	4	5	6
Burk, Anna	70	60	3	4	5
Calder, Ben	100	97	5	6	7
Cooper, Abe	85	87	4	5	6
Fritz, Maria	90	87	4	5	6
Gallante, Susan	100	100	5	6	7
Garcia, Alberto	95	97	5	6	7
Gorton, Becky	65	47	2	3	4
James, Wesley	75	73	4	5	6
Lassiter, Deon	75	77	4	5	6
Lomax, Rachel	60	43	2	3	4
Manning, Trisha	80	87	4	5	6
Moss, Marissa	65	57	3	4	5
Noble, Elissa	100	100	5	6	7
Norton, Tim	85	83	4	5	6
Nunez, Kevin	(fifth grade placement test not given)		1	2	3
Nguyen, Eric	80	87	4	5	6
Potts, Erin	95	93	5	6	7
Sattler, Bill	75	63	3	4	5
Shirey, Jim	100	97	5	6	7
Sattler, Bill	90	87	4	5	6

Making Instructional Decisions

Case Study, Grade 5 (continued)

The second thing Mr. Phelps does is decide on a selection of materials.

- Approaching, on, and beyond level materials are needed.

- He uses the recommendations in the placement materials as a starting point: over 90% indicates beyond level, 80% to 90% indicates on level, and below 80% indicates approaching level materials may be appropriate.

- He will begin instruction with the indicated materials and adjust the materials as he monitors student progress.

- He will also look at the IRI results that indicate Independent, Instructional, and Frustrational levels of vocabulary for each student.

- Mr. Phelps will use the vocabulary levels to help select materials, too, adding extra vocabulary practice for a few students.

Here are his initial reading groups.

Mr. Phelps's Initial Reading Groups		
Group A Working below 5th grade level, with individualizing Includes three sub-groups	**Group B** Working at fifth grade level; using mostly on-level materials	**Group C** Working at sixth grade level; using on level materials and some beyond level materials
Using 4th grade on-level material: Anna Burk Marissa Moss Bill Sattler **Using 3rd grade on-level material** and some 4th grade approaching-level material: Becky Gorton Rachel Lomax **Using ELL materials:** Kevin Nunez	Larry Abel Carol Benz Abe Cooper Maria Fritz Wesley James Deon Lassiter Trisha Manning Tim Norton Eric Nguyen Julie Worth	Ben Calder Susan Gallante Alberto Garcia Elissa Noble Erin Potts Jim Shirey

Making Instructional Decisions

Case Study, Grade 5 (continued)

Progress Monitoring with Ongoing Informal and Formal Assessments

Whole-class and small-group instruction are both used:

- Reading, language arts, spelling, and writing activities are done whole-class.

- Mr. Phelps tries to spend 20 to 25 minutes a day with each small group, during which time he has assigned both individual seatwork and center work (two or three students at a time at one of the four learning centers in the back of the classroom). The students have a list of activities they may do if they finish before time is called.

Learning objectives are used to choose the work for each unit, week, and day. As for the first grade, these objectives are related to the district's curriculum goals and also tailored to student needs as much as possible.

- You have already noted the specific learning objectives for the English Language Learner.

- Mr. Phelps also designs some individual work. For example, he has a plan to strengthen Wesley James and Deon Lassiter's comprehension skills. He knows they get along well and have similar interests, so he has designed some work for them to do during learning center time where they read a story and discuss it together, then work jointly on a story map or other appropriate graphic organizer. This "study buddy" arrangement is a type of flexible grouping.

Ongoing assessments monitor progress on the specific knowledge and skills in the learning objectives.

- Formal assessments in the form of weekly and unit tests, administered to the appropriate groups at the appropriate times, serve this purpose for the whole class and reading group level objectives.

- Mr. Phelps keeps the results of these assessments for both individuals and the group or class. He records the individual grades in his grade book and keeps the test evaluation sheets in students' folders.

- He makes ongoing instructional decisions by noting the strengths and weaknesses indicated by overall performance on weekly and unit tests. In most cases, the decision is to proceed with the next lesson, emphasizing or re-emphasizing some selected objectives during reading groups.

Making Instructional Decisions

Case Study, Grade 5 (continued)

Outcome Assessment

Mr. Phelps feels like he has a good understanding of his students' progress, individually and as a group, from monitoring their progress. As the end of each unit approaches, and as the end of each marking period approaches (these are not always at the same time), he also needs outcome measures. The Unit Tests give outcomes information about learning goals for the unit.

Mr. Phelps had notified parents and students at the beginning of the year about his policies for report card grades. Students knew before any test, project, or assignment if it was just for practice or if it would contribute to their grade. Students had the opportunity to learn and practice before each assessment that formed part of their grade.

For report card grades, Mr. Phelps considers information from several sources.

- The district report card requires that he give grades on an A-F scale for Vocabulary, Reading Comprehension, Writing, and Language Arts. He assembles a set of evidence for each of these.

- For example, he looks at all of the Vocabulary scores from several different quizzes and tests. Each of these is documented (in his gradebook) and could be shown to parents or students if they asked about grades. He makes sure they are on the same scale (he has used the percent-correct scale for each of these scores) before averaging them. He multiplies the more important test grades by two, so they count double, before averaging. Students knew ahead of time what the weight of each component of their grades would be.

Mr. Phelps's grading policy includes an offer that parents who have questions about their students' report cards should call him within one week to schedule a phone or in-person conference. Mr. Phelps usually recommends that the student participate in these conferences.

High-Stakes Testing
Preparing Students for Standardized Testing

Students and their parents should know:

- That a test will be given on a certain date;

- The test's name and what it will cover;

- Why the test is being given; and

- How the results will be reported and used.

Ethical test preparation includes the following:

- Teach the learning goals specified in the curriculum; and

- Teach students test-taking skills.

Teaching the curriculum should result in students being well-prepared for basic skills or state tests.

TEST-TAKING SKILLS YOU CAN TEACH ALL STUDENTS

- Pay attention to directions, both oral and written; ask questions if they don't understand directions.

- Ask how the test will be scored and how individual parts of it will be weighted.

- Write their responses neatly and/or mark answers clearly.

- Study and prepare appropriately (for example, paced studying over time instead of cramming; getting enough rest before a test).

- Use assessment time wisely; work at a reasonable pace; skip questions they can't answer and return to them when the rest of the questions are completed.

- Think before they mark an answer; organize their thoughts before they write.

- Make informed guesses if they don't know an answer (e.g., eliminate choices they are sure are not correct; write partial answers using what they do know).

- Change an answer if they think of a better response.

- Check their work before handing it in.

Accommodations for ELL Students

Accommodations in Assessment

Introduction

Assessments are sometimes changed by using accommodations: changes in assessment presentation format, methods of student response, assessment timing or scheduling, and/or assessment setting. The intention is to allow students with disabilities, Limited English Proficient (LEP) students, or English Language Learners (ELL) to be assessed on the same learning targets as other students. Assessment accommodations are sometimes called assessment modifications.

- Terminology use is changing, however, and some state testing programs use "accommodations" to mean changes in testing conditions that do not change the construct – the concepts and/or skills the test is intended to measure – and use "modifications" to refer to changes in testing conditions that do change the construct. In other places, "accommodations" and "modifications" mean the same thing.

- Teachers who would like to find out more about accommodations in large-scale assessment (for example, for state testing programs) may visit the website of the National Center on Educational Outcomes, a center that specializes in research and policy matters related to the participation of students with disabilities in state and national assessment programs, standards-setting work, and graduation requirements. Their website includes links to research and other resources: **http://education.umn.edu/NCEO/**

Federal legislation requires that students with disabilities must be provided accommodations:

- Section 504 of the Rehabilitation Act (1973)
- Americans with Disabilities Act (1990)
- Individuals with Disabilities Education Act Amendments (1997)
- No Child Left Behind Act (2001)

Accommodations for ELL Students

Accommodations in Assessment

Teachers *want* to provide their students with appropriate accommodations so the students can demonstrate what they know. In some ways, the concept of "accommodations" is just an extension of practices that have been widely used for a long time.

In recent years, educators and legislators have expanded accommodations to include a wide range of student assistance.

- With that has come the question of where to draw boundaries: How much and what kind of assistance or help should be allowed?

- Assistance should be unrelated to the skills and learning.

- Assistance should not mean changing the skills and learning itself. For instance, if you read a passage to a child, demonstrating understanding becomes listening comprehension, not reading comprehension.

The work on large-scale accommodations usually points out two things of particular interest to classroom teachers:

- The need for, and kind of, accommodations should be *documented*. Typically this documentation occurs in the student's Individual Education Plan (IEP) or other individual educational planning documents.

- Students' large-scale testing accommodations should *mirror what accommodations the student has received in these IEPs and in classroom instruction and assessment*.

Both of these principles are equally important, but educators often focus more on the first point and overlook the second. These principles mean that accommodations in assessment and instruction have their foundation in what goes on in the classroom. The large-scale testing accommodations may seem more important, but in fact they are just the logical playing out of the student's IEP, and thus the logical extension of classroom assessment and instructional practices.

Accommodations for ELL Students

Accommodations in Assessment

CTB/McGraw-Hill (2005) accommodations categories:

- Category I accommodations do not change what the scores mean and they are not expected to affect performance level.

- Category II accommodations may affect performance level.

- Category III accommodations include what some states call "modifications." These accommodations are expected to change both the performance level and the skills measured.

For more details about these and other accommodations, you can read the report "Guidelines for Inclusive Test Administration 2005":

http://www.ctb.com/media/articles/pdfs/general/guidelines_inclusive.pdf

---

TYPES OF ASSESSMENT ACCOMMODATIONS

I - ACCOMMODATIONS THAT MAY NOT CHANGE THE INTERPRETATION OF RESULTS (WHAT THE ASSESSMENT MEASURES AND HOW WELL THE STUDENT PERFORMS)

Presentation changes that do not change the task in meaningful ways, for example:

- magnifying glasses, large print
- reading directions aloud or on tape, or via sign language
- using a place marker

Response changes that do not change the task in meaningful ways, for example:

- for selected response items: speak or sign responses or respond with mechanical device
- use spell-checker if spelling is not scored

Setting changes that do not change the task in meaningful ways, for example:

- take test alone or in another setting
- use special lighting, furniture, etc.

Schedule changes that do not change the task in meaningful ways, for example:

- additional breaks that do not add testing time or study opportunities
- changes in time of day or days between sessions that do not add testing time or study opportunities

ELL specific changes

- spell- or grammar-checkers if spelling and grammar are not scored
- computer-based glossary (without content related definitions)
- bilingual word lists or dictionaries
- directions clarified in English and/or in native language (oral and/or written)
- directions translated into native language

Accommodations for ELL Students

II - ACCOMMODATIONS THAT MAY CHANGE THE INTERPRETATION OF PERFORMANCE LEVEL (BUT NOT WHAT THE ASSESSMENT MEASURES); RESULTS SHOULD BE INTERPRETED "WITH ACCOMMODATIONS"

Presentation changes where performance level effects are not known, for example:

- reading assessment material (questions and/or response choices) aloud or on tape, for tests other than reading, or presenting by sign language
- using a calculator or arithmetic tables, for tests other than math computation

Response changes where performance level effects are not known, for example:

- telling responses to a scribe, for tests other than writing

Schedule changes where performance level effects are not known, for example:

- extra time to take the test
- extra breaks or other schedule changes that result in extra time

ELL specific changes where performance level effects are not known, for example:

- reading assessment material (questions and/or response choices) aloud or on tape, in English or in native language, for tests other than reading
- reading assessment material in linguistically clarified English
- responses in native language, translated into English, for tests other than writing

III - ACCOMMODATIONS THAT CHANGE WHAT AN ASSESSMENT MEASURES; RESULTS SHOULD BE INTERPRETED "WITH ACCOMMODATIONS" AND POTENTIAL CHANGES IN KNOWLEDGE OR SKILLS MEASURED SHOULD BE NOTED

Presentation changes that may affect the meaning of what is scored, for example:

- presenting assessment material in Braille
- presenting material via text-talk converter, sign language, or tape recording, for a reading test
- using a calculator or arithmetic tables for a math computation test

Response changes that may affect the meaning of what is scored, for example:

- telling answers to a scribe, for a writing test
- spelling and grammar aides, if spelling and grammar are scored
- using a dictionary, for a writing test

ELL specific changes that may affect the meaning of what is scored, for example:

- reading assessment material (questions and/or response choices) aloud or on tape, in English or in native language, for reading tests
- reading assessment material in linguistically clarified English, for reading tests
- spelling and grammar aides, if spelling and grammar are scored

Note: Accommodations selected and summarized from *Guidelines for Inclusive Test Administration* (2005), by CTB/McGraw-Hill.

© Macmillan/McGraw-Hill

Recording Forms

Name _____ Date

Monthly Instructional Planner (Primary) Record Assessment Results for Grouping Decisions					
	Phonemic Awareness	Phonics	Fluency	Vocabulary	Comprehension
DIBELS					
TPRI					
Fox in a Box					
Informal Reading Inventory					
Placement Test					
Running Records					
Fluency Assessments					
Weekly Tests					
Unit Test					

Recording Forms

Name _____ Date

Monthly Instructional Planner (Intermediate) Record Assessment Results for Grouping Decisions				
	Phonics	**Fluency**	**Vocabulary**	**Comprehension**
Oral Reading Fluency 4-6				
Informal Reading Inventory				
Placement Test				
Running Records				
Fluency Assessments				
Weekly Tests				
Unit Test				

Class Weekly and Unit Test Results

Date																	
Student Name	Wk 1	Wk 2	Wk 3	Wk 4	Wk 5	Unit 1	Wk 1	Wk 2	Wk 3	Wk 4	Wk 5	Unit 2	Wk 1	Wk 2	Wk 3	Wk 4	Wk 5	Unit 3

Class Weekly and Unit Test Results

Date																	
Student Name	Wk 1	Wk 2	Wk 3	Wk 4	Wk 5	Unit 4	Wk 1	Wk 2	Wk 3	Wk 4	Wk 5	Unit 5	Wk 1	Wk 2	Wk 3	Wk 4	Wk 5	Unit 6

Recording Forms

Name _____ Date

Reading Observations Checklist	
Observable Behaviors	**Observed**
Before Reading	
Sets purpose for reading	
Uses prior knowledge and personal experiences	
Previews text or uses text features	
Makes predictions	
During Reading	
Uses metacognitive skills	
Asks questions	
Uses context clues	
Rereads for meaning	
Uses reading strategies	
Revises predictions	
Makes notes or restates information	
After Reading	
Summarizes or retells	
Identifies main ideas or events	
Makes inferences or generalizations	
Analyzes author's purpose	
Uses critical thinking skills	
Responds to text	
Makes connections	

Recording Forms

Name _____ Date

Reading Self-Assessment Checklist			
Reading Behaviors	**How Often**		
Before Reading	**Never**	**Sometimes**	**Always**
I understand the purpose of my reading			
I use what I know or have learned			
I make predictions about what I am going to read			
I look at the title, illustrations, headings, or scan text			
During Reading			
I ask myself questions			
I think about or reflect on what I am reading			
I use context clues or a dictionary for new words			
I reread parts of the text			
I use reading strategies to help me understand			
I change my predictions about what is going to happen			
I make notes or restate information			
After Reading			
I summarize or retell what I have read			
I identify the main ideas or events			
I go back and reread parts of the text			
I analyze ideas and make inferences or generalizations			
I explain the author's purpose for writing the text			
I respond to the text or write something about it			
I make connections between the text and my own life			

Ability Competence in a particular area. Sometimes "ability" is used to mean "aptitude" or "achievement" as well. (See also "achievement" and "aptitude.")

Accommodations Changes to an assessment to allow students with disabilities or English Language Learners to be assessed on the same learning targets as other students; also called **modifications**. Accommodations can occur in the assessment format, methods of student response, assessment timing or scheduling, and assessment setting.

Achievement Competence in a particular area that is acquired as an outcome of learning. (See also "ability" and "aptitude.")

Anchor A sample of student work that typifies a particular performance level. Raters use anchors (for example, anchor papers of student written work) in scoring.

Analytical rubrics A set of rubrics designed to be used together, with a scale of performance levels for each criterion (for example, six-trait writing rubrics score the same piece of writing on ideas and content, organization, voice, word choice, sentence fluency, and conventions). (Compare with "holistic rubrics.")

Aptitude Personal characteristics indicating the ability to develop competence in an area if an opportunity to learn is available. (See also "ability" and "achievement.")

Authentic assessment Assessment that requires students to use combinations of knowledge and skills to do a meaningful task. For example, an exercise about filling in a job application may be considered authentic to a life task.

Assessment Systematically gathering evidence about a student in order to make inferences about what they know and can do. An assessment can include multiple sources of evidence.

Benchmarks Performance descriptions aligned with expected outcomes (for example, state standards or curriculum) for a given grade or level.

Best-work portfolio A portfolio whose purpose is to showcase students' final products or best work in a subject.

Checklist A list of specific attributes of student work, or student behaviors observed during a process, with a place for checking whether the particular item is present or absent (observed or not observed).

Correlation A statistic indicating the degree of relationship between two scores.

Criterion-referenced assessment An assessment for which performance is compared with an absolute standard. Criterion-referenced scores do not tell how a student compared to others, just how well he did in his own right. Example: "John spelled 18 out of 20 spelling words (90%) correctly" is criterion-referenced because it compares John's performance to a standard (20 words). "John got the best spelling score in the class" is norm-referenced because it compares John's performance to others.

Cut score (or cutoff score) A score used to divide performance into categories (examples: mastery/non-mastery; pass/fail; below basic/basic/proficient/advanced).

Developmental portfolio A portfolio whose purpose is to show student growth and progress, sometimes called a growth portfolio.

Diagnostic (diagnosis) Intended to analyze performance for specific areas of understanding and misunderstanding, in order to identify areas for remediation and further instruction.

Distractors The options in a multiple choice item that are not the correct answer. Distractors should be plausible enough to "distract" students who do not have a firm grasp of the concept tested and yet clearly not correct to students who do have a grasp of the concept.

Equivalent forms Different forms of a test that are known to be interchangeable.

Evaluation The process of gathering evidence (assessment) and then using that evidence to make a value judgment about something.

Exemplar A sample of student work at a particular performance level, like an anchor. Some people use the term "exemplar" to mean anchors at any level that are used in classrooms (for example, to illustrate rubric levels for students). Some use the term to mean an example of the highest level of performance.

Formative assessment The process of gathering information that can be used to monitor student progress. (Compare with "summative assessment.")

Formative feedback Information that identifies the strengths and weaknesses of student work in descriptive, not judgmental, language.

"High-stakes" assessment An assessment or assessment program whose outcome has serious consequences, such as a state test.

Higher-order thinking Students' ability to solve problems or use reason. Higher-order thinking is distinguished from simple recall in most taxonomies of educational objectives.

Holistic rubrics Rubrics designed to consider all applicable criteria for scoring at the same time, resulting in one score for the assessment. Using holistic rubrics is faster than scoring with analytical rubrics if all that is required is a final score or grade.

Informal reading inventory (IRI) A method of assessing students' independent, instructional, and frustrational reading levels in which a student reads graded text and answers comprehension questions. Both oral and silent reading can be assessed.

Item One question or exercise on an assessment. Typically, "item" is used to refer to test questions while "task" is used to refer to a performance assessment.

Item analysis An examination of student performance on individual test items, to determine how the item functioned. Two aspects of item analysis include item difficulty (the percent of students who answered the item correctly) and item discrimination (the extent to which an item differentiates between high- and low-scoring students).

Key A list of correct answers used in scoring an objective test.

"Low-stakes" assessment An assessment or assessment program whose outcome does not have serious sequences for students or schools.

Mean The sum of all scores divided by the number of scores in a set; in other words, the "average."

Median The middle score in a set of scores. Half (50%) of the students score above the median, and half score below. Another name for the median is the 50th percentile.

Miscue analysis Recording the kinds of oral reading errors a student makes by looking for patterns in the reading strategies that they use. These strategies are using meaning, syntax, or visual cues to read and understand text.

Mode The score that occurs most frequently in a set of scores; that is, the score that the most students got.

Assessment Vocabulary

National percentile rank A student's **percentile rank** among a national sample of students who took a test.

Norm group The sample of students whose performance on a test was used to establish percentile ranks and other normative information for a test.

Norms A description, usually in the form of tables of percentile ranks, of the performance of a group of students who took a particular test. The set of students is called the "norm group."

Norm-referenced assessment An assessment for which a student's performance is compared with the performance of other students. Norm-referenced scores do not tell how well or poorly a student did something, just how they did in relation to others. See the example under "criterion-referenced assessment."

Objective test (objective scoring) A test for which an answer key can be constructed so that anyone using it would come up with the same score. Multiple-choice, true/false, matching items, and fill-in-the-blanks are examples of objective test items. Sometimes objective tests are called "selected response tests" to emphasize that the student's task is to choose an answer rather than construct one. (Compare with "subjective test.")

Outcomes The results of an educational program. This series focuses on reading achievement outcomes. More broadly, any results of a program can be considered outcomes, including not only achievement but dispositions (interests, attitudes, etc.) and behaviors (for example, future educational choices).

Percent (or percentage) The number correct divided by the total number of items, or the number of points divided by total possible points. Do not confuse this "percent correct," a criterion-referenced score, with "percentile rank," a norm-referenced score (see below).

Percentile (or percentile rank) The percent of students in the norm group scoring below a given student's score. For example, if 60% of students in the norm group scored below a student, then that student scored at the 60th percentile. Percentiles range from 1 to 99. National norms answer the question, "How did this student do compared with children all over the country?" Local norms answer the question, "How does this student compare with peers?"

Performance assessment A form of assessment that sets the student a task requiring either a process or a product (for example, watching a student handle a book or asking the student to write an original story) and rates the performance based on judgment, often with a rubric.

Placement Assigning a student to an appropriate group for appropriate instructional treatment.

Portfolio A collection of student work organized for a particular purpose. Two common portfolio purposes are showing development (for example, a writing portfolio with examples of the writing process and samples from the beginning, middle, and end of the year) and showing best work (for example, a portfolio left on the student's desk for open house). Portfolios can be used mainly for instruction, mainly for assessment, or a mixture of both.

Proficiency level In some states, a category of performance (for example: does not meet/ meets/ exceeds expectations; or below basic/basic/proficient/advanced; or beginning/progressing/proficient/advanced), typically based on a cut score on a standardized test. The term "proficiency level" can also be used to mean how well a student has performed.

Profile A set of scores, often in graph form, for an individual student or group of students (for example, a class). The scores should be expressed in comparable units of measurement to allow comparison and identification of strengths and weaknesses.

Progress Monitoring Using ongoing assessment information to track student growth and achievement against learning targets.

Raw score The number of points earned on a test; for an objective test where each question gets one point, this is the number correct. Raw scores are hard to interpret by themselves, because they depend on the length and difficulty of the test.

Recall Remembering facts and concepts in the same form as they were taught. This type of thinking is assessed by questions that require a student to recognize or identify facts or other information presented or to supply memorized information on a test.

Reliability The consistency or stability of test scores across factors that should not be related to performance. Test scores should not depend on the day or time of testing, or what form of the test is given, or on who scores the test. (Compare with "validity.")

Retelling A method of assessing reading comprehension where a student is asked to recount the story or passage just read.

Rubric A kind of scoring scheme. A rubric is a short (usually 3 to 6 levels), descriptive scale that is applied to student work using professional judgment. The scale level that best describes the work is the one used as the score.

Running record An approach to reading assessment that records a student's oral reading of leveled texts over time.

Scaled score (or scale score) A raw score expressed in units on a continuous scale that makes comparisons between tests, between students, or over time possible. Most standardized tests provide scale scores.

Screening Brief tests to determine which students are at risk for reading difficulties and should be given additional testing for specific diagnosis. Screening can also refer to any testing process that is meant to identify potential difficulties before entering a program.

Self-referenced assessment A student's performance is compared with his or her own previous performance. ("Mai, this paragraph is better than the first one because....")

Standards The term is used for state standards (statements of content and performance expectations) and district standards of achievement of various curricular goals. Some states distinguish between content standards (statements of what should be studied) and performance standards (statements of what level of performance constitutes mastery). "Standard" can also mean a description of performance, as in a criterion-referenced assessment.

Standard deviation A measure of variability of scores. The larger the standard deviation, the more spread out a group of scores is.

Standardized test A test for which the administration, materials, and scoring procedures are fixed, so that student performance can be comparable even when the test is given in different places or at different times.

Subtest A short test that is part of a longer test.

Subjective test (subjective scoring) A test for which judgment is required in scoring. The scorer appraises student work against a rubric based on the level of quality observed in the work. Subjective tests are composed of "constructed response items," so named to emphasize that the student's task is to come up with an answer, not just select one. (Compare with "objective test.")

Summative assessment Assessment that reports on the outcome of learning. Unit tests and other graded work, final exams, and the like are examples of summative assessment. (Compare with "formative assessment.")

Task One question or exercise on an assessment. Typically, "item" is used to refer to test questions while "task" is used to refer to a performance assessment.

Test Usually refers to a paper-and-pencil instrument. Students are asked to respond to a set of items on paper.

Validity The degree to which interpretation and use of test scores reflect intended meaning. Validity is based on the alignment of test questions, tasks, and scoring schemes with their learning targets (this is called "content validity"). (Compare with "reliability.")

More Information

McGraw-Hill Web Sites

Parents, students, and teachers can find resources that coordinate with the stories and other materials at **www.mhschool.com** . Follow the links to "Reading" and then to the student's reading book.

An overview of all of McGraw-Hill's educational products and services can be found at **http://www.mcgraw-hill.com/edu/default.shtml.**